WRITING SHORT STORIES IN SCI-FI, FANTASY, HORROR, AND MORE

FOR FUN AND PROFIT

D. G. AMERICA

Copyright © 2017 by D. G. America, DGA Media.

All rights reserved.

No part of this book may be reproduced in any form or by any electronic or mechanical means, including information storage and retrieval systems, without written permission from the author, except for the use of brief quotations in a book review. All product names, logos, and brands are property of their respective owners and trademark holders and are used as examples only.

Published by DGA Media, version 1.1
ISBN-13: 978-1974560868
ISBN-10: 1974560864

Dedication

To all the storytellers out there: you know who you are.

CONTENTS

Preface — vii

1. Introduction & Author's Notes — 1
2. What Exactly Counts as a Short Story? — 9
3. Short Stories? Really? — 15
4. All Write Already! — 35
5. Done! ...Now What? — 53
6. Read More! — 85

About the Author — 89

PREFACE

I BELIEVE THAT writing short stories in sci-fi, fantasy, horror, post-apocalyptic, and related genres represents a great way to get into indie publishing and finding your ideal readers. Here's my take on why this is so fun, often rewarding, and really exciting.

ONE

★ WRITING SHORT STORIES ★

INTRODUCTION & AUTHOR'S NOTES

Life is an endless collection of short stories.

P*retty deep, huh?* I came up with that myself.

It's true though — think about it. You know that person in your circle of friends who is always the life of the party? That person who as soon as they open their mouths, everyone around stops talking and listens? Why is that? I guarantee that the reason the table goes silent isn't because that person is the richest in the room, or the smartest, or the hottest.

It's because *they tell good stories*.

Think about the last time you caught up with a friend. Maybe you had made plans to meet up for lunch, or you just happened to run into them at the farmer's market. What did you do?

I bet you a million high-fives that at least one of you told at least one story.

Now, when this star of the party or this friend of yours shared their moving tale about how their dog protected a baby duck crossing the road from a stray cat, how long did it take? A minute? Two minutes? *Maybe* three?

When you're talking to someone, you're in a race against time before that person's eyes glaze over and they start to give you the dreaded, "Uh-huh... right... oh yeah?..." which means they are definitely NOT listening. If you want your listener to be interested in what you're saying, you don't have the luxury of setting the scene with flowery language about the color of the sky, or giving a lengthy backstory about how the pond across the street was man-made and a private haven for rich folks back in the twenties.

All your listener cares about in your gripping cat drama is how teeny and cuddly was the helpless baby duck, how close did the cat come to snatching up the fuzzy baby duck, and what the heck was the mama duck doing the whole time her cute duckling was facing imminent danger and certain death??

There you have it: my life, your life, our lives = short stories. (Forget the number 42, this is potentially the meaning of life, folks!)

Boom! (*Mic has been soundly dropped.*)

WHEN MOST PEOPLE think of writing, they get overwhelmed, thinking they have to come up with some epic, intricate tale about faraway kingdoms or galaxies that spans generations.

Hello?!? What about Isaac Asimov? Shirley Jackson? Ray Bradbury? Ursula K. Le Guin?

Sure, these folks all wrote novels too, but their

short stories have been among the most influential and powerful additions to the sci-fi, fantasy, and horror genres.

What I'm getting at with all of this, is that short stories are rarely given the respect they deserve, and they're a lot closer to our natural way of communicating than full-length novels. They're also a great way for a new writer to dip their toe in the proverbial hot spring and see if this whole writing thing is for them. Even if you've already published works in other genres, if you're trying to break into the world of fantasy, sci-fi, or horror, writing short stories is still a safe bet, as readers of these genres are historically much more accepting of this medium than, say, readers of romance or mystery.

This book is all about how short stories can open doors into the writing world that might otherwise stay stubbornly closed if you stick solely to full-length novels. Short stories can be:

- **Less Intimidating** — Shorter stories make for more manageable goals.

- **More Flexible** — Because short stories can (usually) be written faster than full-length novels, they result in a more prolific book portfolio, which can be used in a myriad of ways from straight up sales, anthologies, giveaways, or even ghost writing for hire.
- **Very Instructive** — There's nowhere to hide in a short story; it has to be crisp, tight, and thoughtful. Writers of any experience level can benefit from honing their storytelling skills in the short story realm.
- **Fun and Profitable!** — (Yes, the subtitle of this book!) Writing in general can be a lot of fun, and with the growing industry of independent publishing, also referred to as self-publishing, writing short stories in particular can provide you with an additional revenue stream.

A Brief History of Me

So who am I, anyway?

I'm a life-long sci-fi enthusiast who can rarely get through a day without quoting from either *Star Wars* or *Star Trek*. I'm the guy who, when I went to stay in China for four months, knew my girlfriend at the time was the one for me when she mailed me the *Lord of the Rings* trilogy (and yes, I know it's not *really* a trilogy). And I'm the one who watches *The Walking Dead* but has sworn not to tell said girlfriend (now wife) anything about it because it's "too creepy" for her.

More importantly, however, I'm an experienced (but always improving) author with several short stories and full-length books already published — both under my own name and under assorted pen names — in paperback, ebook, and audiobook formats across multiple platforms. I currently have books and more for sale on Amazon, Apple iBooks, Barnes & Noble, Kobo, Google Play Books, Tolino, Scribd, 24Symbols,

Inktera, Gumroad, OverDrive, Audible, and others.

I've got a boatload of knowledge about the self-publishing industry, and I'm eager to share it with you. Why? Because there can never be too many good books in the world!

Alright, that's enough about me. Let's get to the good stuff…

TWO

★ WRITING SHORT STORIES ★

WHAT EXACTLY COUNTS AS A SHORT STORY?

Let's talk about how much you actually need to write. While you'll get different numbers pretty much everywhere you look, the generally accepted labels based on book lengths are approximately:

- Short story: 1,000 - 7,500 words
- Novelette: 7,500 - 20,000
- Novella: 20,000 - 40,000
- Novel: 40,000+

Many science fiction and horror full-length novels tend to stay in the range of 50K to 75K words, but fantasy can be as much as 80K or higher, sometimes well above 100K words. But we're focusing on the other end of the spectrum.

There's also a growing interest in flash fiction, which is usually defined as less than 1000 words (think Andy Weir's amazing 999-word *The Egg*).

How do these word counts equate to actual pages? Great question! Simple. The standard page of text is between 100 and 300 words (double-spaced), or about 500 words (single-spaced).

Not so scary, right? If you write 300-500 words today, you've already written an entire page of your story. You could write your first 3000-word short story simply by writing the equivalent of only six pages of single-spaced text!

But remember, don't feel chained to these numbers. They're just useful as a rule of thumb. If ending your story at 7,500 words would feel forced and create a bad reader experience, by all means, keep writing. These are only guidelines, and no one will complain if your short story could *technically* be considered a novelette.

How is a Short Story Different?

While the difference between a short story and other forms of writing may seem obvious, length is actually only one of the defining factors. Style of writing and story structure are key elements as well.

The standard structure for a full-length novel — and often novellas and novelettes — is the three-act structure. Whole books have been devoted to breaking down this structure, so here's the bird's eye view:

- ACT ONE — introducing your main character/setting/problem
- ACT TWO — putting your main character through the wringer
- ACT THREE — your character either solves the problem or dies

And in these writing forms — novels, especially — there's abundant room for description and exposition, plus opportunities for multiple points of view from different characters.

A short story, however, doesn't typically use this kind of 3-act structure, nor does it have the breathing room for pages and pages of world building.

Laser focus on one event, one character, even one scene is what short stories are all about. Details about the world and the characters are incorporated on a need-to-know basis only. That's the magic and challenge of shorts!

Longer writing forms also often choose one or two broad themes to explore in depth, using all the tools at hand — symbolism, plot points, character perceptions, etc. — to leave the reader thinking about those themes in general terms.

Take the *Harry Potter* series, which focuses on (among others) the themes of the power of love, the nature of real family, and the seductive allure of tyranny. After you read one of these books, you definitely walk away with a heightened awareness of these themes, but every reader will view them through the lens of their own lives and experiences.

Short stories, meanwhile, are often about a single

question or hypothesis. You — the author — have a specific message you want to communicate to the reader. When they put your book down, they should be able to sum up in a single statement what that story is about.

For example, Isaac Asimov's *The Dead Past* is about the morality of the centralization of scientific research. To explore this concept, Asimov creates a scenario that forces every reader to ask themselves the same question at the end of the story: "Was the government right to have kept the truth secret for so long?" That simple question leads to other inevitable questions like, "Do the benefits outweigh the detriments?" and "Is it even possible to pursue knowledge without it somehow being exploited?" And even though everyone will have a different opinion, no one can read this story without asking the question that Asimov sculpted the story to ask.

Sure, there are short stories that are written and read strictly for entertainment purposes — a fun, scary romp through a world we visit for half an hour or forty-five minutes. And if that's the kind of story you want to write, go for it.

Your best stories are going to be the ones you'd love to read, and whether that's thought-provoking sci-fi, skin-crawling horror, or urban fantasy, you can bet that someone else in the world would love to read it too.

I could go on and on about the power of short stories, but countless books by much more qualified authors than me have been written about this art and craft, so I'm not going to delve much deeper here.

Just keep in mind that short stories are short (duh!) but not too short, focused more on action than description, and usually revolve around a single thesis or question.

Think of a compelling character, an interesting impossible situation, decisions made or to be made, and a short narrative brimming with real emotion. Then you have a story. The kind that will keep readers turning the pages of your books or e-readers!

So that's the *what*, now let's talk about *why*...

THREE

★ WRITING SHORT STORIES ★

SHORT STORIES? REALLY?

But is this really a good use of my time, energy, and creativity?

Yes, really!

Short stories meet that magic requirement of the two simple truths for all creative people, including writers and aspiring authors:

1. You have to start.
2. You have to start somewhere.

No one's saying writing truly compelling short stories is easier than crafting full-length novels; in fact, there are probably plenty of people who would argue it's harder.

But the fact is, for a lot of people, writing short stories takes much less time than completing novels, and for many people time is THE determining factor in whether you finish, or whether you throw up your hands and walk away from the blinking cursor forever:

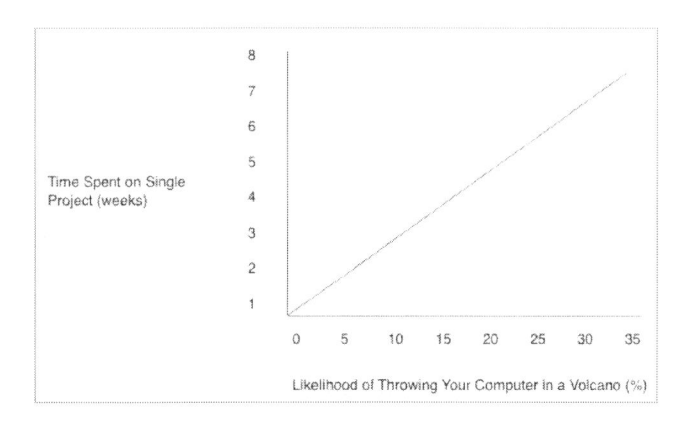

[Chart: Time Spent on Single Project (weeks) vs. Likelihood of Throwing Your Computer in a Volcano (%), showing a linear positive relationship]

See? It's science. (source: *The Journal of American D.G.*)

You still have to get your butt in the chair. You still have to fire up the laptop and write your very best. (By "write your very best," I of course mean write a crappy first draft. Nobody writes their "very best" until the third or fourth edit and polish!)

But short stories are one of the most effective ways to ease into the world of writing, and into the world of sci-fi, fantasy, and horror specifically. Why? Because...

Shorter Lengths Make for Manageable Goals

Let's say you have a great idea for a book. Maybe right now it's just an interesting character, plot point, or world, and you'd love to dive in and explore more about this idea of yours in a full-length novel. However, if you're like most of the human population, your day job, your family, and other obligations already keep you busy enough, and the task of writing a novel seems so daunting and time consuming that you never even begin.

Now your idea, which could have been the next Big Thing, has been lost. Set aside. Put in a drawer. Lost on your hard drive. Fading away on a restaurant napkin.

Think back on the previous chapter, and about your 3,000-word story goal. It's only six pages folks! Do you think you could write six pages within the next, say, month? Of course you can! (We all can!)

A friend of mine who's a freelance copywriter has been dreaming of writing his big epic novel for over a decade, but always felt too busy writing sales copy for newspaper, radio, social media, and television ads.

We met for lunch while I was writing this book (BTW, panini sandwiches are extraordinary, I must say!), and I told him about this new approach I was trying with short stories. He was so fired up, that within a couple days he had already started writing his own. Now he's able to get about one story a month done between his copy jobs. He has an Amazon publishing account, and is finding readers and selling his short stories. And he couldn't be happier.

Need help starting? It's about details, images, scenes. When I mentioned lunch before that was generic. But if I mention a tomato basil mozzarella panini, I'm being more specific and setting the scene for two writers having lunch.

We all have ideas. All day and all the time. Just grab one and decide that you want to build on it. What if that sandwich shop had live music?

So take that lone idea for a story and add a little to it. What would happen if your main characters stumbled upon a rock band consisting of animate, evil dolls? Or what if that silent, noiseless world was suddenly filled with an achingly beautiful song, or music that turned everyone into superheroes? Just remember to keep it simple: What do you want the reader to be thinking when they finish your story? What question should they be asking themselves?

A short story is also a more manageable length when it comes to asking friends, family members, partners, or others to read it and offer their thoughts.

If you drop a 100,000-word first draft novel in their laps and say, "Call me when you're done!" you may not ever get any feedback because your beta readers are busy with their lives too. Short stories that can be read in a day are much more likely to be finished, and then you can capture that endangered and elusive creature: useful feedback.

Lots of Stories = Lots of Ways to Find You

Short stories are also really useful to help you find new readers. It just makes sense: the more works you have available for sale, the more opportunities a reader has to find you. Of course, given the choice between ten awful books and one stellar book, you'd rather have the latter, but the goal here is to have as many different avenues through which a reader can find your books as possible.

If you wrote one 80,000-word novel, that's awesome, and congratulations! But it's still only ONE product.

Even if a reader does find it, read it, and love it(!), there's nothing else of yours available, so that reader's going to leave and possibly never come back.

Contrast that with the ten 8,000-word short stories you could have written during that same period. If a reader finds just one of your titles, they still have NINE other products of yours to read (and buy). Think of each story as a "highway" into your catalog. If you only have one highway that leads to you, and then once a reader arrives, there isn't even a decent coffee shop in town, they'll probably just leave.

We'll get into the profitability of short stories later in this chapter, but most 80,000-word novels are priced around $2.99 or $3.99 in ebook form. Even though short stories aren't usually priced more than $0.99, if someone buys all ten, you'll get more than double what you would have with the novel!

Of course, you could just split the difference by writing a single 50,000 novel and six 5,000-word stories for the same 80K words of output, productivity, and storytelling. I'm not saying that this plan would take the same amount of time as a single 80,000 word novel, but you get the idea!

I know for a fact that this strategy works, because I've followed this path as a reader many times. When I stumble across a new author, I always look in their library to see if they have a short story before buying one of their full-length novels. This gives me a window into the author's writing style, ensuring that it's a match for me before making the commitment to their longer works.

I have also discovered some of my favorite new writers in short story anthologies and tracked down the rest of their catalog to see what else they've written.

Short Stories Can Help You Focus on What Works

Sometimes it's hard to know if a premise, character, plot, or world is enough to merit a full novel or not — both from a content point of view, and from the realistic sustainability of my own interest. While I may be captivated by the story right now, I know myself well enough to understand that I may not love it as much six months from now.

Always starting with the goal of a short story removes the pressure of having to make the novel vs. short story decision too early, and it allows me to tell a quick tale and then leave it behind while it's still fresh and energizing.

Even if you do think an idea is rich enough for a full novel or even a series, you might be the only one. It's nearly impossible to tell which of your stories will gain the most attention, and therefore which deserves to be expanded. Leaving that up to the readers is a great way to keep guesswork out of the equation.

This is what is sometimes called *writing to market*, where you focus your writing in that sweet spot where reader demand and your interests intersect. And while no one is going to stop you from only writing your passion projects, knowing where the interest of real buyers — and therefore the potential for new readers — can be very motivating.

So if you come up with a story or idea that you think could warrant further exploration, but don't want to waste time on a potential goose egg, feel free to leave a note for your readers, asking for their input:

> "Final line of magical short story."

THE END

Thanks for reading this short story! Want to read more about Sunny, the guitar-playing homicidal rag doll? Let me know by leaving a public review HERE [with link]. I'm always happy to read your feedback, and reader interest helps me prioritize my project schedule. Thanks again!

Or something to that effect.

Adding a note like this at the end of all of your stories accomplishes two things: instead of just hoping for readers to review your work, you're openly asking for it, and we all know that reviews are to readers what headlights are to possums: once they see them, they're probably not going anywhere. (That's a thinker, and if you don't get it, just consider it a statement of American oddity that you can ignore.)

The other thing it does is make the reader feel valued (best not tell them we likened them to possums — hey, we're all readers anyway, right?). Telling your readers that their feedback is critical in determining which stories get explored further makes them feel more involved in the process. Then, when you do release *Sunny II: Shredding at the South Pole*, they'll be among the first to buy it.

Getting your work out in the marketplace earlier rather than later is also an invaluable way of getting honest (often brutally so) feedback on your writing skills and creative muscles. No matter how much they sting, those one-star reviews that call your dialogue forced, your pacing slow, or your characters shallow, can reveal genuine holes in your developing craft that need attention.

Of course, some reviews are just plain ridiculous — I've seen one-star reviews because the buyer couldn't figure out how to get the title on their device! But grab a craft beer, set your ego aside, and read all of them, because you're sure to learn something.

And by the way, there's no rule that says you have to write under your real name. I've got more than one pen name, and it's remarkably liberating to know that I can write anything I want without the public being able to trace it back to me. If you want to write super dark, grotesque and shocking contemporary horror, but are worried your boss or family will find out and look at you differently, or that people will see bad reviews and think you're a horrible writer, go ahead and write as Darky McHorror (if you use that name, you're welcome!).

Short Stories Can Make Money. For Real!

We already noted the pay difference between having one full novel and multiple short stories, but let's dive even deeper into their potential for profitability.

As of this writing, the most popular Science Fiction & Fantasy short story in Amazon's Kindle store (a 45 minute read, approximately 22-32 pages long) has a 4,658 sales rank in the entire paid Kindle store. Using KindleSpy, a Chrome app for estimating an author's monthly earnings based on sales rank, that book is probably getting about 850 downloads/sales per month, resulting in a monthly revenue of $842, or roughly $295 in paid royalties (35% for a $0.99 ebook).

My wife and I have a running gag when one of my early, not-so-great-actually-crappy books brings in paltry change in an entire month. When I mention the sorry number, she says, "If I saw a dollar and ten cents [or whatever the dismal amount is] in the driveway, I'd pick it up." Well, if she saw $295 in the driveway, I'm pretty confident my wife would pick that up too.

Not bad for a single short story — and that's only one, priced at $0.99. Imagine what you could get with five stories, a dozen, or an anthology!

If you're still not convinced, think about all of these well-known movies that have been made from short stories:

- *The Boogeyman*, Stephen King (basically anything by Stephen King!)
- *The Fly*, George Langelaan
- *It Had to Be Murder*, Cornell Woolrich (became Alfred Hitchcock's *Rear Window*)
- *The Minority Report*, Philip K. Dick (again, pretty much anything by Philip K. Dick)

- *The Sentinel*, Arthur C. Clarke (*2001: A Space Odyssey*)
- *Supertoys Last All Summer Long*, Brian Aldiss (*A.I. Artificial Intelligence*)
- *Arrival*, Ted Chiang

And that's only a handful of what's out there. The short story form leaves open plenty of room for on-screen extended character development, stunning cinematography, and thrilling soundtracks! Your short story could be the Next Big Thing — but only if you write it!

Alright... we're drifting back down to reality now... We'll write our Academy Awards speech later. Before your short story becomes a blockbuster film, let's get back to discussing the here and now.

The going rate for a single short story, as an ebook, is $0.99. Of course, the platform you're publishing on is going to take its cut of the back end for the access to customers, the website, all of the credit card processing, the delivery to the customer's account, and any after-sale customer service.

On Amazon (KDP), you'll earn a 35% royalty on ebooks priced less than $2.99, which means on a $0.99 book you'll get a whopping $0.35 for every story you sell.

No, this is not a lot of money.

Yes, the subtitle of this book does say something about "profit."

But, we've already seen the power of having multiple short stories available as opposed to one full-length novel and how that can pay more in the long run. And that's only counting each short story as one isolated product. One of the amazing features of a short story is that it is far more flexible than a full-length, 80,000-word novel because you can combine your titles into bundles or anthologies.

Here's just one example:

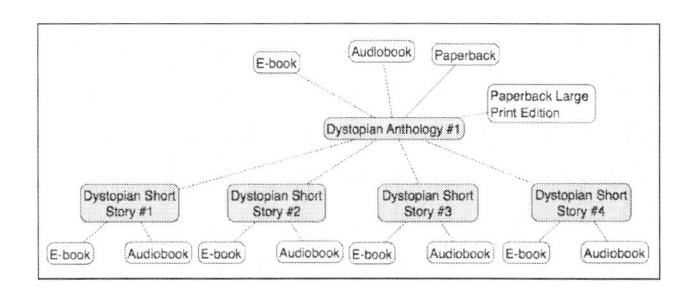

After writing just four short stories, you now have TWELVE products available for sale! And the anthology is going to be priced accordingly, at $2.99 or even $3.99. You can't typically produce paperbacks with a single short story, since it's highly unlikely you'll meet the minimum page count (24 pages for Amazon's CreateSpace) for printing. But then again, a 7,500-word short story at 300 words per page is 25 pages, so it's possible once you add a title page, copyright page, author bio, and more — and definitely with a large print edition — which would bring your product count up to TWENTY (two more products per short story)!

And that's assuming all of your short stories are similar in some way. Let's take a look at a different scenario where there are more short stories that are more varied in subject:

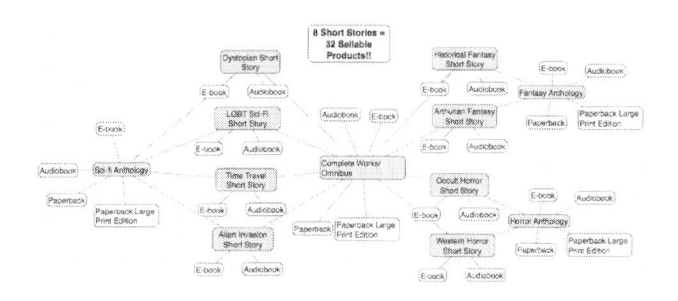

Your eyes are not deceiving you, my friend: THIRTY-TWO products from eight short stories! I counted three times, just to make sure. And that's not counting paperbacks of the individual short stories (because, frankly, it's doubtful anyone would buy those — but you never know!).

Now, to be fair, if you were to write eight novels, you'd also get thirty-two products (four different versions of each book). BUT which is going to take longer? I'm guessing the eight novels, how about you?

Would you rather have thirty-two short story products out in — let's be overly conservative — two years? Or thirty-two novel products out in — let's be overly ambitious — four years? I vote the former. (Of course, mix and match these two strategies as you see fit!)

Also, you really can't do anthologies with novels — at least not in a paperback version, since they'll likely be too long. (You could probably get a series of three, maybe four short novels, into a single paperback, but the printing limits would keep you from adding more than that.)

Yes, there are some "novel" anthologies for sale online. You see them all the time, with twenty different books by multiple authors. But these aren't actually full-length novels — they're short stories or novelettes (usually prequels) that introduce a reader to a new series. And rarely do these products have any audiobook or paperback editions.

Demand is High

Why would a reader buy a short story when there are so many full-length novels in your genre available? Honestly, some won't.

This means that as you continue to write your 3,000 to 7,500-word stories, you will be compiling them into anthologies where readers can buy — or borrow (more on that later) — your collections of stories. You can experiment with different genres, different themes, or you can just lump all of your writing together.

And as your craft and storytelling gets better, you might want to add a novel to the mix to draw in all those readers who found you through your short stories.

In the meantime, remember that bestselling short story we mentioned earlier? That book wouldn't be making a killing if there wasn't anyone around who wanted to read it. The demand for bite-sized fiction is out there.

Whether a reader wants a sample taste of an author's writing style as I mentioned earlier, or they're just not the kind of person to commit the 100 hours or so that it takes to read George R. R. Martin's *A Song of Ice and Fire* series, there is an audience for your short story!

FOUR

★ WRITING SHORT STORIES ★

ALL WRITE ALREADY!

Oh, what a terrible pun. I love it.

Anyway, now that you're thoroughly convinced short stories are the way to go, it's time to start writing.

How do you get started? The nuts and bolts of your writing routine are going to be unique and different from everyone else's, but if you're new to writing, here are my five "easy" steps for getting the ball rolling:

1. Be passionate about the genre as a fan. The longer you've been reading, watching, and consuming sci-fi, fantasy, or horror, the more familiar you'll be

with the existing tropes, ideas, and trends, keeping your stories fresh and interesting.
2. Come up with a story idea, scene, or premise. Jot it down somewhere, anywhere, and then dive in.
3. Get your first draft done. Don't worry about language or word count, just get that first draft FINISHED.
4. When you're ready — preferably at least a week after you've finished the first draft so you're going into it with fresh eyes — write, scrub, edit, expand, shrink, and get your more polished second draft done. If you can't afford an editor, give it another week or two and then do this again, and again a week or two after that. Go ahead and let a few friends or relatives look at it too. Fix any problems, and then PUBLISH! (Later when you get fancy, get more books out, and start making money, then go ahead and use a paid editor and possibly even some beta readers by giving away advance copies to some of your more avid fans.)

5. Be realistic. Don't compare your first (or recent) attempts at storytelling against the masters in the field (you only get better by writing more!). Be critical, but be objective. If your story is fun, interesting, and it works — from the perspective of a reader now, and not as the picky writer — then publish it. If you're still nervous, then roll it out under a pen name and get to work on the next one.

Habits

Whatever your writing routine ends up being, try to stick to it. It's a well-known fact that if you actively engage your creative mind at approximately the same time every day, and under similar circumstances (e.g. in the morning with your first cup of coffee or tea in hand, or late afternoon in the same noisy cafe), your brain will take the hint and start to switch on automatically once the proper signals (the taste of your drink, the sound of the espresso machine) are received.

Start small. Give yourself a daily word count goal

of, say, 500 words. You can keep track of your word count in a number of ways, whether it's a built-in feature of your writing software (like in Scrivener — more on that later), an external app (like Pacemaker Planner), or that old standby the spreadsheet. Of course, if you're in the zone and don't want to stop at 500 words, by all means write on! This is a goal only, not a limitation.

The habit of tracking word count first attracted me through the simple math of it all. My own personal goal is to write 2,000 words per day (like the great Stephen King!), or the equivalent of four single-spaced pages (or eight double-spaced pages).

Writing 2,000 words a day even just 5 days a week — go ahead and take the weekends off if you want, I won't tell! — gives you a 10,000-word story draft, or two separate 5,000-word stories each week. Even 100 words a day is a 3,000-word short story each month. Thinking about all of that was enough to get me hooked.

Here's a snapshot of my writing productivity from the beginning of 2017 that I keep in a tracking spreadsheet on Google Drive:

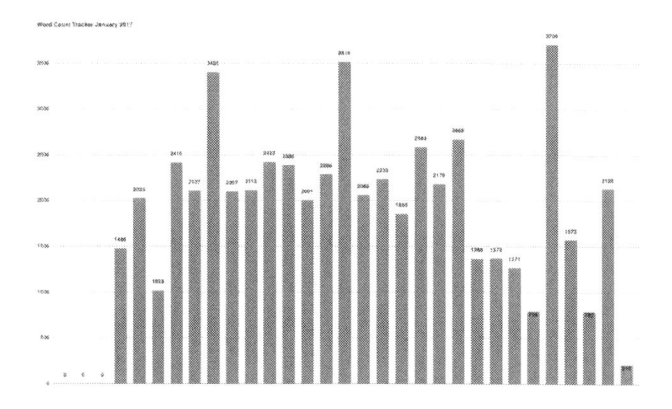

You can see my best day in the month, surrounded by a few days that were crazy busy with life stuff. But even though I had days where my wonderful life got in the way, I still managed to hit my 2K per day goal for much of the month (after coming back from a family trip around New Year's.)

I can tell you that this habit of tracking output by word count has really helped me step up my writing, and instead of worrying about anyone else (that includes you, Mr. Amazing Stephen King), I just compete with myself and my own stats. This totals over 56K words for the month of January, a new record for me!

If that sort of production schedule — even 500

words per day — sounds too aggressive at the beginning, that's fine. But once you make a habit of tracking your daily word count, and you start to see those daily and monthly totals add up, your writing speed is almost guaranteed to accelerate. Grab a notebook, a journal, make a spreadsheet, whatever, but make a goal and stick to it.

Using Sub-Genres as Inspiration

Perhaps you really want to write, but you're drawing a total blank on ideas. Or maybe, if you're like me, you've got far too many ideas, which — believe it or not — can be just as stifling as having none. Either way, if you're struggling with what kind of story to write, getting a better sense of the landscape is a great way to unlock your imagination.

As you know, every genre has its own sub-genres, which are constantly evolving and expanding as readers continue to follow their varied interests in specific tropes, character types, and plot expectations. And — for the entrepreneurial writers among us — each of these sub-genres has its own dedicated top 100 best seller sales list on sites like Amazon, making it easier for readers to find the most popular picks in their favorite book genre.

Browsing these sub-genres can be extremely useful both as pure creative inspiration (hmm... writing a steampunk sci-fi short story could be fun...), or to get a sense of where the opportunities are (...I wonder how many books would need to exist before they create a new "animate toys" horror sub-genre?). If you're careful and strategic about how you launch your book, using specific categories and keywords, you can send it right into the hands of those hungry, eager readers of your intended sub-genre.

Here are some of the available **science-fiction** choices for readers and writers alike:

- sci-fi adventure
- alien invasion
- alternative history science-fiction
- anthologies & short stories
- colonization sci-fi
- cyberpunk science-fiction
- dystopian sci-fi

- first contact sci-fi
- galactic empire science-fiction
- genetic engineering
- hard science-fiction
- LGBT sci-fi
- metaphysical & visionary science-fiction
- military sci-fi
- post-apocalyptic
- space exploration
- space opera
- steampunk sci-fi
- time travel
- *and more*

The most impressive thing about this list is that it is not only incomplete in many ways, but it is fully organic. What this means is that over time, if enough books, authors, and readers flock to a sci-fi specialty (same goes for fantasy and horror), it's entirely possible to help create a new sub-genre and category.

These sub-genres are not necessarily story prompts, but they can almost work that way. Instead of sitting down with the intention of just writing a science-fiction story, which is a very broad goal and kind of scary for some people, ask yourself: Do you have a military sci-fi short story idea? Can you imagine a cool twist on space exploration?

For **fantasy** stories, it's the same scenario. There are so many categories and sub-genres — each presumably with its own audience — that you can write in. Here's a sampling:

- alternative history fantasy
- fantasy anthologies & short stories
- Arthurian fantasy
- Christian fantasy
- coming of age fantasies
- dark fantasy
- epic fantasy
- fairy tales
- historical fantasies
- LGBT fantasies
- metaphysical & visionary fantasies
- myths & legends
- new adult & college fantasy
- paranormal & urban fantasy
- superhero fantasy
- sword & sorcery

- *and more*

For **horror**, it's a little more complicated, because — at least on Amazon — the category is nested under the "Literature & Fiction" list rather than having its own spot like the "Science-Fiction & Fantasy" or "Mystery, Thriller, & Suspense" categories.

Some other book/ebook vendors lump horror into sci-fi & fantasy because of the many overlaps (i.e., post-apocalyptic, dystopian, dark fantasy, etc). But here are the categories in horror, each with its own top 100 best seller list, both free and paid:

- horror anthologies
- British horror fiction
- horror comedy
- dark fantasy horror
- LGBT horror
- occult horror
- short stories
- U.S. horror fiction
- western horror fiction
- *and more*

It's interesting that in horror, anthologies and short stories are separate lists. And with the generally shorter sub-genre list, you can see the potential opportunities for new categories. All it takes is readers, writers, and books to converge in a new spot.

But how can you create a new sub-genre if you can't select that category to release your book?

Keywords, my friend, keywords.

Your setting (e.g. Antarctica, colonial Virginia, etc.), character types (animate doll, politician), character roles (strong young adult female, independent senior, cyborg), plot themes (revenge, forgiveness, coming of age), or story tone (comedy, romance) can be used as keywords, and in turn help identify category and sub-genre.

While my romantic comedy horror about Sunny slashing his way around the South Pole may not be broad enough to become a sub-genre in its own right, over time you can see how a number of horror stories set against a military backdrop could create a new category — if there are enough of them, and enough reader (i.e. buyer) interest.

And if you're careful with your choice of keywords and categories, it's possible for your single book or story to be cross-listed across several ebook categories. Here's a screenshot from one such book:

```
Look for Similar Items by Category
  • Books > Science Fiction & Fantasy > Science Fiction > Colonization
  • Books > Science Fiction & Fantasy > Science Fiction > Cyberpunk
  • Books > Science Fiction & Fantasy > Science Fiction > Exploration
  • Books > Science Fiction & Fantasy > Science Fiction > Galactic Empire
  • Books > Science Fiction & Fantasy > Science Fiction > Hard Science Fiction
  • Books > Science Fiction & Fantasy > Science Fiction > Military > Space Fleet
  • Books > Science Fiction & Fantasy > Science Fiction > Military > Space Marine
  • Kindle Store > Kindle eBooks > Science Fiction & Fantasy > Science Fiction > Colonization
  • Kindle Store > Kindle eBooks > Science Fiction & Fantasy > Science Fiction > Cyberpunk
  • Kindle Store > Kindle eBooks > Science Fiction & Fantasy > Science Fiction > Galactic Empire
  • Kindle Store > Kindle eBooks > Science Fiction & Fantasy > Science Fiction > Hard Science Fiction
  • Kindle Store > Kindle eBooks > Science Fiction & Fantasy > Science Fiction > Military > Space Fleet
  • Kindle Store > Kindle eBooks > Science Fiction & Fantasy > Science Fiction > Military > Space Marine
  • Kindle Store > Kindle eBooks > Science Fiction & Fantasy > Science Fiction > Space Exploration
```

Collaborate

If you're just starting out, you should simply start writing as much as you can on your own and learn as you go. But since I've been publishing for a while, I've grown to understand the power of collaboration. You can collaborate with other writers in a number of ways:

- <u>Mastermind Group</u> — Generally you won't be eligible to join a group like this until you've got some successful books under your belt. But I spent an entire year in a mastermind group with three other authors and indie publishers, and while it was a serious commitment (two hours every week), I learned a lot. The most experienced in the group was regularly making 4 to 5 figures every month from his publishing. Beware "mastermind groups" that charge you to be a member. You may still learn something, but it's really just a way of lining someone else's pockets with your hard earned royalties. If you do participate in a group like this, you'll want like minds at similar stages in their writer (and publisher) journeys.
- <u>Writing Group</u> — Do you have a friend who is also interested in writing stories? If so, you can start a writing partnership where you hold each other accountable for meeting goals, inspire healthy competition, and serve as the first line of defense against that deadly disease:

giveupitis, sometimes referred to as *Quit-Too-Early Syndrome*. If you start to feel frustrated and ready to give it all up, your writing partner can boost your spirits with a pep talk or just good old plain blackmail ("If you don't finish this chapter, I swear I'll post that picture of you with the mullet!").

- Co-Write — And if said friend of yours writes stories in the same genre as you do, you could easily bundle your stories together and perhaps even down the road co-write and co-publish novellas, novels, or a complete series together. If you dig around on Amazon, you'll see a number of author collaborations that look quite successful based on output and sales rank: Colin Barnes with Darren Wearmouth; Michael Anderle with Justin Sloan, Craig Martelle, T.S. Paul, or Paul Middleton; Sean Platt with Johnny B. Truant or David Wright, and others. Working together gets more books out faster, gets your readers to cross-pollinate, and just improves discoverability overall.

Tools

What tools do you need? There is a lot of software available with the sales pitch that it will help you write efficiently and effectively. Just like everything else for sale, some of it is genuinely helpful, and some of it is simply more time spent away from the blank page. But the reality is, there's no way for you to know what you need or what software could be helpful until you start writing and figure it out. Just open Microsoft Word or Apple Pages and begin. (Or grab a yellow legal pad, you rebel!)

Once you've got a first draft under your belt, then you can start to think about what kinds of tools would be useful for you. Did you find yourself constantly opening and referencing files that are separate from your draft file? Then maybe Scrivener would be helpful, since you can include those files inside the Scrivener file.

Were you often distracted by (the-oh-so-evil-time-suck-of) social media? Maybe Focus is the right app for you, which can block a number of websites for a specified amount of time. (This is a

Mac app, but there are several similar apps available for Windows too.)

Is it hard to tune out the noisy din of your surroundings? Perhaps Noisli or Brain.fm would be beneficial, each of which plays customizable background sounds, noises, or music to block out the world around you.

Even if you think one of these would be helpful simply based on the description, wait until you've sincerely identified it as a recurring problem before spending that hard-earned cash that you picked up in your driveway on it. (Well, Noisli is free, but both Focus and Scrivener cost money.)

With all that said, here are a couple software programs and apps that I use regularly that you may find beneficial as well down the road:

- Aeon Timeline — $$ This is a project management software that revolves around — you guessed it — creating timelines. There are several different pre-made templates, including one specifically for writers, which has built-in features to track characters, places, and story arcs. One of the coolest aspects about this program is that it tells you exactly how old a character is at any given point on your timeline. While that might not seem so revolutionary, if your story includes time travel, or flashbacks, it can be really useful seeing everyone's age during a certain event at a glance. This program might be overkill for short stories, which tend to be simpler in scope, but if you're going to write a novel, or several short stories that will be in a common world or part of a related series, this might be a good fit.

- <u>Scrivener</u> — $$ I've already mentioned this program a bunch in this book, and that's because it's incredibly useful for writers. You can do your own research on it when you're ready, but it's essentially a combination of a file folder and Pages (or Word). Not only do you have the capability of writing in Scrivener, but as I mentioned before, you can store files related to your writing project *inside* the Scrivener file, all visible and readily available. It also has a heap of features designed to make writing easier, including color coding, cork board view, and word count tracking. For less than $50, it's well worth the money, but there can be a steep learning curve to take full advantage of the power of this tool, so you have to be willing to commit the few hours to watch some tutorials.

These are just a handful of the many useful tools available. But remember, as cool as they seem, and as tempting as it may be to let the tools "make you a better writer," you don't need to spend any money to write. Just write already!

Oh — you've already got something written? You're just not sure what to do next? Well, I can help you with that too…

FIVE

★ WRITING SHORT STORIES ★

DONE! ...NOW WHAT?

Some authors don't have any problem writing their stories, but get stuck on the steps that are necessary to publish their ebooks, paperbacks, and audiobooks, and make them available to readers.

Even if you plan on hiring someone to take care of all of this for you, this chapter is well worth reading, if only to understand the mechanics and what you'll be paying for. (Once you see how easy — and expensive — it can be, you may change your mind and want to manage the publishing process yourself!)

The Basics

The simplest way to understand what is required is to realize that once you have your story written, here's what else you need:

For Ebooks:

- a high-quality, high-resolution ebook cover image (jpg or tiff)
- an interior file of your text formatted specifically for ebook readers (the standard formats are mobi and epub)

For Paperbacks:

- a high-resolution 300 dpi PDF interior file
- a high-resolution 300 dpi PDF full-wrap cover file with spine

For Audiobooks:

- 192 kbps or higher mp3 files at 44.1kHz separated by chapters

- separate open and closing credit mp3 files and a retail sample
- a cover image at 2400 x 2400 pixels in JPG, PNG, or TIFF format greater than 72 dpi

If you have no time, interest, or understanding of this process, you *can* outsource these steps to others. You can use sites like fiverr.com, upwork.com, and others to find help. Or do a quick search for "ebook formatting" or "ebook cover design" on your favorite search engine.

After you've outsourced a couple times — and spent your panini money — you might be inclined to learn about the conversion process and either do your own ebook/paperback formatting, or design your own book covers, or both. These are not difficult things to learn, and if you have limited funds to start with (before you make any sales), at least try to do your own formatting.

As we saw earlier in this book, there are typically four types of sellable products related to each title:

- ebook
- Paperback
- Paperback — Large Print Edition
- Audiobook

Unfortunately, these don't just spring into existence as soon as your short story is done, and you're going to have to spend some money one way or another to get them published. If you are motivated to learn about best practices for indie publishing, there are so many tools, resources, video tutorials, and more available online. After having spent many hours watching these videos and listening to podcasts myself, here's the glad-I-learned-this stuff, including initial steps and other useful resources that I really believe can help you.

Ebook Formatting

Your goal is to convert your text into mobi or epub formats with a linkable TOC (table of contents). There are several ways to do this, including straight from Word, Pages, or even Google Docs.

Scrivener — even though it's a writing app — can also create ("compile") ebooks in both formats, but I can't talk about formatting without talking about an awesome tool called Vellum. As of this writing, Vellum is only for Mac (frowny face if you're a PC person, but there is Mac-in-Cloud!). Go ahead and read about it though, because maybe it will be enough to convince you to switch!

I'm in a bunch of writer groups on Facebook, and a while back, a lot of the other members were giving glowing reviews about this Vellum program, so I checked it out. When I saw how pricey it is ($200-$250), I thought, "No way. I can format my ebooks just fine in Scrivener." (It was a pain and a half, but I was stubborn.)

After a few more months, I kept seeing the name Vellum pop up in euphoric posts about saving "so much time" and how "gorgeous my ebooks are now!" So I went back and poked around again. It definitely looked interesting, but I still couldn't make myself bite the bullet.

I actually wrote to the guys who made the software (two former Pixar employees) and asked if they were planning on having any sales, or if they had a referral program I could participate in. They wrote back and said something like, "This program will change your life. It's already cheap!" (I'm paraphrasing. Actually, they were super nice, and I've corresponded with them more than a few times since, and they're always very professional and receptive to my feedback.)

Finally I got fed up with the time consuming and cumbersome process of formatting books in Word, Pages, G-Drive, or Scrivener, and just bought Vellum. Believe it or not, the hype was completely warranted, and it really was worth the money. It's amazingly well-constructed software that does nice table of content integrations, drop-cap styling, and more.

If you're not going to generate your own ebooks (although you should), then you don't have to worry about it, but after you spend fifty to a hundred bucks each time you hire someone to format your ebook, you're definitely going to want to check this program out for yourself.

You can always hire someone to do this for you, but Vellum is surprisingly easy to use, and I can't recommend it enough. Whichever formatting program you decide on, spend the time and watch some videos to learn how to do it right. I usually search for "[program] ebook formatting 2017" to get the most recent videos for any best practices.

BTW, I don't get any money by recommending Vellum, but if you're not convinced, this book (ebook and paperback version) was formatted in Vellum... and it looks SWEET!

Paperbacks (including Large Print) Formatting

The most important part of the paperback formatting process is choosing the right trim size, or dimensions, of your book. Paperback fiction can vary widely in size, and it really depends on the length of your book.

If it's a single short story, you're going to want it to be small, to make the spine thicker (for example, 5x8 inches). But if it's an anthology of all your works, you'll want to go with a larger trim size (6 x 9 in), so it's not crazy thick.

You need a PDF to create a paperback, and

obviously Word, Pages, Scrivener, and even Vellum can create interior PDFs for you. Adobe InDesign is usually what a professional book designer will use, however I've known some professional, successful authors/publishers who create their paperbacks in PowerPoint! Any program that can output in PDF format can get you there.

A few of the aggregator platforms themselves also have built-in paperback formatting services. For example, Draft2Digital will make a rough conversion to epub/PDF from any DOC, DOCX, or RTF file that you can use on their site and even download to use elsewhere.

Now let's make a second paperback! In order to create a Large Print paperback for readers with visual challenges, you need to make the font size and style as easy to read as possible. According to a page on the American Council of the Blind website, the following are some of the rules that should be applied in order to qualify for the *Large Print* label:

- <u>Font Size</u> — at least 18 point font, preferably 20-24 pt
- <u>Font Style</u> — bold, sans serif, mono or fixed-space font
- <u>Line Spacing</u> — at least 1.5 (leading)
- <u>Titles and Headings</u> — larger than the document text, and left-justified
- <u>Preferred Fonts</u> — Verdana, Helvetica, Tahoma, Arial, and others

Be sure to make it very clear that this is a *Large Print* edition, by including it on both the cover image of the paperback and the title information on the sales listing.

Once you have your PDF, you can upload a cover and interior file for your book on CreateSpace (another Amazon-owned company), or at sites like Ingram-Spark, Nook Press, or Lulu.

In the old days before the mighty pterodactyls roamed the skies, you would have to get hundreds of copies printed and then hope people would buy them. (Can you say cases of books in the closet, basement, and garage?) Now, CreateSpace and other vendors will keep the file on hand, but won't print anything until there is an order (on Amazon or elsewhere). This is called "print on demand," and it's incredibly liberating, as it allows for revisions and re-uploads even after your book has gone live (more on that later). And no stacked up inventory!

Audiobooks

For audiobooks, you'll need clear, high-resolution audio files, which you can either do yourself, or hire a voice actor to do. Unless you have access to a good microphone, a recording studio, or your house is in a really quiet neighborhood and you can hide away in one of your closets, this may be one thing that's easier to subcontract.

Not only do you need to record the audio (which could take hours depending on your reading skill and the length of your story — and you better have a pop filter to take out all those hard consonants), but you need to mix and master it, which requires not only software but some know-how. That said, Audacity is one of the most popular tools for recording, mixing, and mastering your own audiobooks, and although there is a learning curve, there are — as always — a ton of free tutorials on YouTube to get your started.

Amazon owns ACX (Audible), and ACX has an easy-to-use platform for finding the right narrator for your story. Once your book is published on Amazon, you claim your book on ACX, upload an audition sample of the text, and then select the specifics that you're looking for in a narrator, including gender, language, accent, voice age, and vocal style. (I've got one sci-fi story narrated by a fantastic woman from South Africa. Her accent was perfect for the futuristic nature of the story.)

There are a number of options you can choose for each category. For example, here are some of the available accents:

ACCENT					
☑ Any					
☐ American-General American		☐ British-Glasgow		☐ Hispanic	
☐ American-Boston		☐ British-Liverpool		☐ Indian	
☐ American-Mid-West		☐ British-Manchester		☐ Irish-Southern Irish	
☐ American-New York		☐ British-Northern English		☐ Irish-Dublin	
☐ American-Southern		☐ British-Northern Irish		☐ Irish-Cork & Kerry	
☐ American-Urban		☐ British-Welsh		☐ Irish-Cavan	
☐ American-Western		☐ British-West Country		☐ Italian	
☐ Asian Other		☐ British-Yorkshire		☐ Japanese	
☐ Australian		☐ British English-Newcastle		☐ Middle-Eastern	
☐ British-General British		☐ Canadian-English		☐ New Zealand	
☐ British-General Scottish		☐ Canadian-French		☐ Russian	
☐ British-BBC English		☐ Caribbean		☐ Scandinavian	
☐ British-Birmingham		☐ Chinese		☐ Spanish	
☐ British-Cockney		☐ Eastern European		☐ South African-Afrikaans	
☐ British-Edinburgh		☐ French			
☐ British-Essex		☐ German			
☐ British-Estuary		☐ Greek			

And here are some of the possible vocal styles that professional narrators and voice over artists can bring to the reading of your audiobook. (Don't think it matters? There can be big differences between *brooding*, *inspirational*, *announcer*, and *spooky* styles. Don't worry. Your voice artist will help you decide if you're not sure.)

Once you post your text sample and state your preferred price per hour of finished audio (or royalty split with no upfront costs!), voice actors/narrators on ACX who are interested can upload their audio file auditions of your sample. Not only do you get a taste of their voice and style, you can also judge the quality and clarity of the audio they upload.

A quick warning: When listening to the narrator auditions, beware of computerized voices. ACX will only allow book narrations by humans. No computer programs or auto-readers are tolerated, and use of them will be a breach of ACX's terms of service. It doesn't happen often, but I have had scammers submit auditions for some of my stories, and even though it's subtle, I could tell the voice reading it was an auto-reader. If ACX determines that your narrator isn't human, your entire account could be jeopardized, and at the very least your book will be rejected. You may be able to convince them you were an unwitting victim, but best not to chance it.

Covers

Covers are THE single most important aspect of your book. Covers sell books. They do. End of story.

Most publishing platforms often feature cover creator utilities, but I've always found these to be limited, and the results below the standards of most ebooks. It's fine to be indie published, but you don't want to look like it!

There are websites where you can hire designers, such as Fiverr, Upwork, 99designs, and others. Another common solution is to purchase pre-made ebook covers where the design and layout has already been set and you simply submit your title, author name, and other information to the designer to customize your cover when you buy it. This can range in price from very cheap ($15-$25), to very expensive (up to a few hundred dollars or more for one cover!).

Here's a list of some of my favorite pre-made ebook cover sites. If they aren't clickable on your device, just type them in and check out what's available:

www.thebookcoverdesigner.com/shop/
www.goonwrite.com
www.designsbyrachelle.net/store/c6/Pre-made_ebook_Covers.html
www.yocladesigns.com/pre-made-covers
www.tomedwardsdesign.com

If you don't find what you need, or aren't impressed by the cover selection at those sites, most of the designers represented there will do custom work for you starting from scratch. You could also just go out on your favorite search engine and look for "book cover designers" or "pre-made ebook covers," and you'll find even more choices.

Because of how tricky finding the right cover can

be, many authors actually buy the cover first — or at least early on in the writing process — and use it as a guide for their story. This strategy eliminates the looming fear that you'll have to spend hundreds of dollars on a custom cover, since you already bought the perfect cover for a fraction of the cost!

Buying the cover first can also be useful in a couple other ways:

- The entire project feels more real, and it's possible to tie the story into details you see on the cover that you might not have imagined otherwise.
- Because of the financial commitment it takes to get a cover, whether pre-made or custom, already having a cover can help motivate you to actually finish the story. No one wants to spend money on a cover that they never use, even if it was only $35. That story is almost guaranteed to be one that you finish — even if only to validate the expense!

If you are a skilled graphic designer with Adobe

Photoshop, InDesign, Affinity Designer, or other related programs, it's fine to make your own ebook covers in the beginning, especially if you're trying to save money.

Most design software is available for a one-time purchase, but Adobe has an online subscription service called Creative Cloud which gives you access to all of their applications for a single monthly fee (with an education discount for teachers and students, in case this applies to you). This can be a great way of learning the tools as you go.

Just be sure to compare your cover design results to the other published covers in your genre. Without a half-decent or professional-looking cover, most readers won't even give your book a chance.

The art requirements for ebook covers, paperback covers, and audiobook covers are all different, as noted earlier. Be sure to check the specifications on each platform for each product cover before hiring a designer, so you both know what you need and you won't waste your money or their time.

Where Should I Publish? (KU vs. Going Wide)

There are many, many platforms where you can publish your book: Amazon, Apple, Google, Kobo, Barnes & Noble, as well as international platforms like 24Symbols, Xin Xii, and Tolino — and that's going directly to the marketplaces. There are also numerous aggregators, or distributors, where you upload your title once, and they distribute it to multiple platforms for a small cut of the royalties. Some of the better known aggregators include Draft2Digital, Pronoun, and Smashwords.

Think about where you bought your most recent ebook or book. Chances are it was on Amazon. It is by far the largest platform, and there are plenty of authors who make a living publishing exclusively on Amazon.

If you enter your book in their Kindle Select, Kindle Unlimited (KU) program, readers can borrow your title without actually buying it, and you get paid for every page they read. This feature, however, comes with a catch: you can't publish your title on any other platform while it's in KU. All content that's in KU must be available only on Amazon (exclusive!), or else you're breaching their terms of service (TOS) and risking your entire Amazon publishing account. There are some other platforms that have similar borrowing programs, but again, Amazon is the most popular.

KU isn't always a great fit for single short stories because of the low page count. The best strategy for us short story authors is to wait until you have an anthology, and put that in KU (to get the high page reads). The rest of your single short stories — the one's that AREN'T in the anthology, otherwise they're not exclusive to Amazon and breaking their terms of service — can be sold on Amazon and the other different platforms, creating more inroads to your work.

But remember, as soon as you put a short story in an anthology and are planning on entering it in KU, you MUST remove it from all other platforms. Even if you have it for sale on your own personal website, Gumroad, or a Shopify store, you have to take it down, otherwise it's not exclusive and it's against Amazon's rules. (Yes, I know I just said that a in the last paragraph... and in the paragraph before that... but I can't stress this enough. You DON'T want to lose your Amazon publishing account. This is the biggest marketplace in the world, and if you lose access to Amazon, you're going to have a much harder time making it as a writer.)

But here's a positive to Amazon's serious dedication to ebooks. For short stories, Amazon is a good match, with their specific "Short Reads" category:

> ‹ Any Department
>   ‹ Kindle Store
>   Kindle Short Reads
>   15 minutes (1-11 pages)
>   30 minutes (12-21 pages)
>   45 minutes (22-32 pages)
>   One hour (33-43 pages)
>   90 minutes (44-64 pages)
>   Two hours or more (65-100 pages)

This category offers readers a chance to dip their foot into a topic (non-fiction) or story (fiction) and finish reading in a single sitting. Short Reads is an ever-growing category, with more than $200,000 estimated royalty revenues for the top twenty best sellers alone (as of this writing):

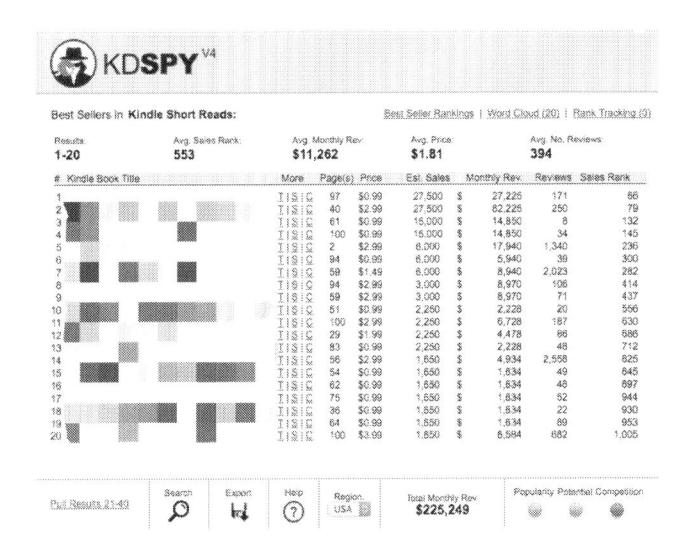

Because Amazon is available as a shopping platform in dozens of countries across the globe, once your new ebook goes live, it automatically becomes available to readers on thirteen Amazon stores: USA, United Kingdom, Canada, Germany, Spain, France, Italy, Netherlands, India, Japan, Australia, Mexico, and Brazil. And readers in other countries often shop directly on the main Amazon USA site. This means that when your book goes live — generally within 24 hours of being uploaded — your stories can be accessible to readers all across the globe.

Guess Who's Excited about Translations!

One of the most amazing, fascinating, and exciting opportunities for new authors is foreign language editions of their stories and books.

Years ago, foreign language book translation was largely limited to bestselling authors with the big-five traditional publishers or certain academic imprints. Foreign markets were considered a luxury.

Accessing these locations around the world was something that either organically happened — much later in the process — or because a foreign language publisher reached out to you and offered a licensing deal and they took care of the new edition.

But let's talk about the real possibilities of indie publishing growth of ebooks, paperbacks, and audio in the coming years. It's a big, big world, and sure plenty of the world's population speaks English, but how many other readers could you have across the globe — and even in the United States — if you took your stellar science-fiction, fantasy, and horror books to other languages?

The major languages that Amazon itself promotes as "Foreign Language" ebooks are:

- Chinese
- French
- German
- Italian
- Japanese
- Portuguese
- Russian
- Spanish
- *and other languages*

Each of these foreign language categories has its own free and paid best seller lists, very often across the same categories as the massive English-speaking ebook store. And these are just the major foreign language categories. Amazon supports books written in over thirty languages, from Welsh to Norwegian to Icelandic. I've taken advantage of this opportunity under my pen names, with books translated into Spanish,

French, Portuguese, Italian, and Danish editions. One book actually sells a lot better in Spanish than in English!

Wait, did you say Danish?

You bet! I had a request out for different language translations, when a very articulate, friendly, and professional translator reached out to me because of that gig. I was hesitant about spending money on a Danish translation, until I did some of my own research.

Roughly 5.6 million people around the world speak Danish, in many countries other than Denmark: Germany, Canada, Iceland, Greenland, Norway, Sweden, the United Arab Emirates, and the USA.

Seemed like enough for me to take a chance on a couple small projects. Especially since reading ebooks hasn't even become mainstream across the globe yet. Even in the United States, only about 28% of Americans say they've read an ebook, and 14% listened to an audiobook in the last twelve months before a recent Pew Research Study.

So how can you take advantage of this

opportunity? Step one is to write, edit, and release a handful of your stories.

Maybe even wait on getting a translation until you have a collection or anthology, because you'll probably get a better deal from the translator if you have a big bundle of work at once, versus several little projects spread across a year.

Step two is to look on Craigslist, Upwork, or another reputable work-for-hire website (probably best not to go with Fiverr, as the quality/professionalism may not be as high as you need it to be, but you never know now that they're rolling out Fiverr PRO), and post your gig.

Don't be afraid to haggle, but don't take advantage of people either — if your translator feels like they're getting the short end of the stick, you may not get the best product back.

It's also often worth paying another translator/editor who is fluent in both English and your selected language to edit the book after it comes back from the first translator. This may sound expensive, but if you're going to the trouble to get the first volume of your omnibus translated, you definitely want to make sure it's representing you correctly. And once you find a solid translator whose work always passes muster with the editor, you can trust them with future projects and skip the second pair of eyes.

A Few More Foreign Language Opportunities

I already mentioned earlier in this book the myriad sub-genres that are available under the Science-Fiction, Fantasy, and Horror categories. But... that was in English.

If you go to Amazon (the US store) and look under the Foreign Languages category and select a language, you'll see that most of the languages listed have only one umbrella category (and therefore one top 100 best seller list) called Fantasy, Horror, & Science Fiction:

> ‹ Kindle eBooks
> ‹ Foreign Languages
> Chinese
> Arts, Film & Photography
> Biographies, Diaries & True Accounts
> Business & Economics
> Children's eBooks
> Comics & Manga
> Cookbooks, Food & Beverages
> Crime, Thriller & Mystery
> Fantasy, Horror & Science Fiction
> Historical Fiction

Breaking into a broad list like that, especially when the first page is bound to be filled with JK Rowling and other blockbuster authors, is going to be nearly impossible. But if you write enough stories in a specific sub-genre and get them translated, then use smart, leading keywords, you might eventually be able to create a new sub-genre in this language that will almost exclusively feature your work!

For some languages, however, this umbrella category isn't as impervious as it seems. Take, for example, the Chinese Fantasy, Horror & Science

Fiction category pictured previously. Look at how many paid best sellers are listed:

> 1-20 21-32
> About Best Sellers in Fantasy, Horror & Science Fiction in Chinese

That's right: thirty-two! (And by the way, as of this writing, #32 on the list is a short story!) So if you write a story in fantasy, horror, or science fiction and get it translated into Chinese, you're almost guaranteed a spot on that best sellers list on Amazon's US Kindle store!

Focus on Writing, Not Marketing...

Many new authors write a single story or novel and watch it disappear into the abyss for sales after launch — and that's assuming there was some nominal interest from friends and family upon release. While this can be quite disheartening, the thing to remember is that this is normal.

It is VERY difficult to get traction on a first book — especially a single short story — by a new author. While there are ways of getting attention for your book, they're pretty much all expensive, and they'll be a waste of time if you only have one short story for sale.

Your goal should be writing your stories, not marketing them. Go ahead and set up a mailing list on MailChimp, AWeber, or Madmimi, and put a link to it on your author bio page and in the backs of your books, but don't do more than that.

Don't worry about marketing until you get your first anthology together. Once that's available for sale, that means you've got a wider variety of products that will appeal to a wider variety of readers — both those who want short stories and those who want something longer.

I know an indie author who spent $175 on a marketing campaign on a single standalone 35k-word novella. He had two other books available for sale, but in wildly different genres than the one he was promoting, and he had no mailing list. So he was essentially starting from scratch. The minuscule amount of exposure, traffic, clicks, sales, and page-reads that he got for that $175 was "almost silly" (his words).

Since he had already spent $125 on his ebook (not great) cover and complained at the time about the exorbitant cost, he would have been better off spending that additional $175 (marketing money) on a much more compelling cover or even his next cover. Or he could have at least waited to promote until he had another project for happy readers to buy even if they did find and love his book.

The bottom line is: marketing is often a distraction, especially without a backlist. Don't worry about it at first, and just keep writing more fantastic stories!

... Except Your Mailing List

The second most important thing for a writer to have is a mailing list. (Can you guess what the first is? ...No, not creativity, although that is critical... No, not caffeine, although that comes in handy when you were up half the night making the final touches on your latest story... Yes! Persistence! This takes time. Lots of time. George R. R. Martin, for example, was writing for more than thirty years — including several short stories, by the way — before becoming a household name.)

Anyway... as I was saying, a mailing list will be your most powerful promotion tool, and it's one of the few marketing strategies that you can set and forget, and will just keep working for you until you're ready to use it. This is the best way to communicate directly with your fans and spur sales of your stories when they're released.

A popular and very effective way to get people to sign up for your mailing list is to give them something in return, such as... a short story! Yes, many successful authors reel readers into their mailing lists by offering them an exclusive short story that is only available to those who sign up. As a short story author, you're uniquely qualified to provide this carrot for your readers.

The key word here, however, is *exclusive*. You cannot give away a short story that is already for sale, unless you want to make people angry. Think how you'd feel if you bought everything by one of your favorite authors (like me!), then saw that you could get another short story by them for free just by signing up for their mailing list, only to find out that it's something you've not only already read, but paid for? I'm thinking you'd be not so psyched.

Also, if the short story you're offering people is also in Amazon's Kindle Unlimited program, you're breaching their terms of service by not keeping that material exclusive to Amazon.

Final Thoughts on the Production Process

I spent money on tools like Adobe Creative Cloud, Affinity Designer, Scrivener, and Vellum only after I started making money. I have also regularly re-evaluated my catalog, and have seen a bump in sales when I refresh a few early ebook covers and formatting attempts. But remember that whether you hire someone to help or do it all yourself, the writing is the most important part of all of this.

If you don't have a great product, it doesn't matter how spectacular your cover or your formatting is. Write your best, and the readers will find you.

SIX

★ WRITING SHORT STORIES ★

READ MORE!

I know you're supposed to promote your own works in your own books, but I'm going buck the trend and use some space to promote books by other writers (and no, this isn't paid advertising — I've never even met these guys!) whose books on writing have helped me.

Here's my recommended reading list of books on writing:

- 2k to 10k: Writing Faster, Writing Better, and Writing More of What You Love, by Rachel Aaron (Very inspiring book by a funny author whose underlying motto is: Love what you write, and it'll be easy.)

- How to Write Short Stories And Use Them to Further Your Writing Career, by James Scott Bell (His descriptions about short story writing are so on the money!)
- 5000 Words Per Hour: Write Faster, Write Smarter, by Chris Fox (We're all shooting for a higher level of production, and that comes from tracking. Great series of books around writing sprints. There's even an iOS app to help. Also check out his other great books on writing like *Write to Market*.)
- On Writing: A Memoir Of The Craft, by Stephen King (A classic, filled with funny and inspiring anecdotes. This guy knows how to tell a story... obviously.)
- Bird by Bird: Some Instructions on Writing and Life, by Ann Lamott (Another classic that's also hilarious.)
- Write. Publish. Repeat. (The No-Luck-Required Guide to Self-Publishing Success), by Sean Platt and Johnny B. Truant (A book by the guys who run the

Self-Publishing Podcast, which set me onto a better long-term plan of production.)

It's also always really inspiring to go back and read your favorite short stories — while you find new ones. If you're as big a fan as I am, you've probably read all these already, but here are some of my favorites:

- *The Martian Chronicles*, Ray Bradbury
- *This Long Vigil*, Rhett C. Bruno
- *Stories of Your Life and Others*, Ted Chiang
- *The Lost Colony*, Josh Hayes
- *Night Shift*, Stephen King
- *The Compass Rose*, Ursula K. Le Guin
- *The Slow Sad Suicide of Rohan Wijeratne*, Yudhanjaya Wijeratne

Hopefully by now you're fired up about writing short stories for sci-fi, fantasy, and/or horror, and you've found some value here.

But this book also has a hidden value to you as a yardstick. Why do I say that? Because when all is said and done, this book (~12,700 words) is about the length of two short stories. Flip through when you're done and re-evaluate the length and realize that you can (easily!) do this with your word count!

Lastly, make sure that you check out all the amazing podcasts on YouTube and iTunes by indie authors. There is so much useful (and free) stuff out there by people doing this every day. And seriously, read those recommended writing books and THANK YOU again for reading mine.

Best of luck with your writing and self-publishing journey, and remember to make sure you're having fun!

ABOUT THE AUTHOR

D. G. America is an emerging author of post-apocalyptic fiction, sci-fi, and more. He lives near Boston, and he's ready.

THANKS FOR READING THIS. PLEASE CONSIDER LEAVING A REVIEW WHERE YOU FOUND THIS BOOK!

For more information:
amzn.to/2fLP7l5